Comic Relief

Comic Relief

Drawings from the Cartoonists Thanksgiving Day Hunger Project

FOREWORD BY KENNY ROGERS
INTRODUCTION BY GARRY TRUDEAU

AN OWL BOOK
HENRY HOLT AND COMPANY/NEW YORK

Published by Henry Holt and Company, Inc.,
521 Fifth Avenue, New York, New York 10175.

Published simultaneously in Canada.

Library of Congress Catalog Card Number: 86-80716

ISBN 0-03-009093-8 (pbk.)

First Edition

Designed by Jeffrey L. Ward
Printed in the United States of America
10 9 8 7 6 5 4 3 2 1

ISBN 0-03-009093-8

Contents

Foreword xiii
Introduction xvii

Adam 10
ADventures 76
Agatha Crumm 13
Alley Oop 18
The Amazing Spiderman 61
Amy 83
Animal Crackers 52
Annie 29
Apartment 3-G 78
Archie 79
Arlo and Janis 27
Arnold 55
Ask Shagg 25

Babyman 7

Barney Google and Snuffy Smith	84
B.C.	19
Bears in Love	65
Beetle Bailey	16
Belvedere	34
Benchley	25
Ben Wicks	83
Berry's World	37
The Better Half	60
Betty Boop and Felix	66
Bizarro	21
Blondie	86
Bloom County	52
Boner's Ark	24
The Born Loser	63
Brenda Starr	46
Brick Bradford	82
Bringing Up Father	11
Broom Hilda	89
Brother Juniper	26
Bugs Bunny	90
Buz Sawyer	39
Caldwell	15
Calvin and Hobbes	48
Captain Easy	27
Captain Vincible	9
Cathy	11

Cheeverwood 19
Conrad 75
Cooper 43
The Crass Menagerie 22
Crock 28

Dick Tracy 51
Dollar$ and Nonene 87
Doonesbury 79
Downstown 54
Drabble 4
Dr. Smock 43
Duffy 88
Dunagin's People 12

Eb and Flo 77
Eek and Meek 32
Ellie 14
Elwood 38
The Evermores 74
Executive Suite 45

Family Circus 8
Farley 58
The Far Side 5
Fenton 57
Ferd'nand 49
Flash Gordon 33
For Better or For Worse 78

Frank and Ernest 59
Fred Basset 66
Funky Winkerbean 42

Garfield 75
Gasoline Alley 2
Geech 58
Gil Thorp 89
Gino 30
The Girls 71
Good News—Bad News 53
Grimsly 41
Grubby 14
Gumdrop 64

Hägar the Horrible 2
Hartland 82
Hazel 15
Health Capsules 87
Henry 40
Herman 26
Hi and Lois 72
Howie 3
Hubert 36

It's Just a Game 56

John Darling 39
Judge Parker 74

Kit 'n' Carlyle 68
Kudzu 77

Laugh Time 47
The Lee Way 30
Leotoons 23
Little Farmer 88
The Little Man 71
Love Is . . . 68
Luann 73
Luther 33

Mandrake the Magician 67
Marmaduke 12
Marvin 61
McGonigle of the Chronicle 20
Middle Ages 59
Miles to Go 45
Miss Peach 32
Momma 62
Moon Mullins 3
Moose Miller 51
Motley's Crew 6

Mr. Abernathy 31
Mr. Men & Little Miss 28
Jim Henson's The Muppets 54
My Grandma . . . 21

Nancy 18
The Neighborhood 80
Nubbin 81

Off the Leash 34
On the Fastrack 38

Pavlov 37
Peaches 85
Peanuts 49
Perky and Beanz 73
. . . Pero Pa' Lante! 42
The Peter Principle 53
The Phantom 69
Ponytail 50
Popeye 22

The Quigmans 50
Quincy 86

Return with Us to Caring 47

Rex Morgan, M.D. 91
Rip Kirby 72
Robotman 4
Rose Is Rose 16
Rudy 48

Sally Forth 13
Sam and Silo 70
Secret Agent Corrigan 81
Shoe 29
The Small Society 35
The Smith Family 91
Snake Tales 31
Sons of Liberty 64
Steve Canyon 10
Steve Roper and Mike Nomad 7
Stockworth 40
Stumpy Stumbler 63
Sugar 85
Sydney 20
Sylvia 35

Tank McNamara 65
Tiger 9
Tim Tyler's Luck 24
Today's World 8

Trudy 80
Tumbleweeds 84
Twitch 55
Tyler Two 90

Ug! 69
The Underground Surrealists 46

Vidiots 56
Village Square 76
Virgil and Company 62

Wee Pals 57
Willy 'n Ethel 23
Winetoons 41
Winnie Winkle 60
Winston 36
Winthrop 70
The Wizard of Id 67
Wright Angles 6

Ziggy 5

Editorial Cartoons

Tony Auth (*Philadelphia Inquirer*) 17
Paul Conrad (*Los Angeles Times*) 1
Bill Day (*Detroit Free Press*) 44

Foreword

by Kenny Rogers

All of us involved with USA for AFRICA are grateful to the *Comic Relief* cartoonists—especially Milton Caniff, Charles Schulz, and Garry Trudeau, the organizers of the project—for donating their time and talent to the hunger effort. The Cartoonists Thanksgiving Day Hunger Project last year was a major success; and now, with the publication of this book, many more people will have the chance to share in these artists' inspiration, and in the spirit of USA for AFRICA.

Several years ago, when I first became actively involved in hunger issues, I immediately became aware of one thing. No one really wants to know about world hunger—

because if you know it exists, you know you have to do something about it, and that isn't easy.

But I also saw that hunger is a problem that concerns everyone; if you can't personally empathize with the hungry, you can still sympathize with them. What's more, people want to help. They want to feel that they've made a dent in the problem, that they've accomplished something. All they need is the opportunity.

For many of us, USA for AFRICA has provided that opportunity. A little over a year ago, we started with a song—"We Are the World"—and a lot of hope. Since then, USA for AFRICA has become a movement of worldwide proportions. From single individuals to entire communities, people have worked together to create a whole much greater than the sum of its parts. We watched as eight-year-old schoolchildren broke open their piggy banks and gave their pennies; we listened on Good Friday, 1985, as thousands of radio stations across the globe played "We Are the World" simultaneously and crowds gathered in front of St. Patrick's Cathedral in New York to sing along. As one of the artists fortunate enough to have sung on "We Are the World," I can say that the response has been truly humbling.

As I'm writing this, USA for AFRICA is preparing for the ultimate participatory event: Hands Across America. This May, when over five million people clasp hands in a single line, stretching more than four thousand miles from coast to coast, it will be one of the most significant moments in American history. We will raise millions of dollars for

America's hungry and homeless—but even more important, we will again witness the incredible power generated when people from every imaginable walk of life come together for a single cause.

Comic Relief is another example of that power, as well as a testament to the talent and commitment of the artists involved. When you sit down and read all of these strips together—with their humor, their poignance, their messages of hope and concern—you cannot help but be moved. And that, after all, is what USA for AFRICA is all about.

Introduction

by Garry Trudeau

Sneaking up on your average big-time, twentieth-century American cartoonist requires a certain forbearance. Traditionally, cartoon creators are somewhat withdrawn (except for Mike Peters), taciturn (except for Mike Peters), and casually dressed (except for Winsor McCay, but he's dead). All of which makes them pretty hard to spot, especially since they are frequently sequestered under deadline for weeks at a time. On those rare occasions when cartoonists do venture out, it is almost always to play golf on weekday mornings. We have our share of party animals, of course, but they rarely congregate any place with a working sign out front.

Personally, I never viewed peer inaccessibility as problematic until last summer when

Charles Schulz, Milt Caniff, and I pooled our directories and set out to get the collective attention of our colleagues. As letter after letter was rebuffed as undeliverable, we began to wonder how many royalty checks must be languishing in syndicate escrow accounts. Moreover, the average sixty-day response time to those of our letters that *were* delivered did not bode well for the project.

Until, that is, we read the responses. It is a remarkable tribute to the power of the cause that support for the Cartoonists Thanksgiving Day Hunger Project was close to unanimous. (The only cartoonists unable to participate were the small handful who had already completed the work on their features for that day.) Last Thanksgiving, over 175 artists, inspired by the potential impact of a concerted effort among their ranks, did something they had never attempted before—they worked together. In so doing, they moved millions of people to focus their attention on a tragic, *preventable* problem of tremendous proportions—world hunger. It is our profound hope that this modest expression of concern will be both instructive and contagious.

Comic Relief

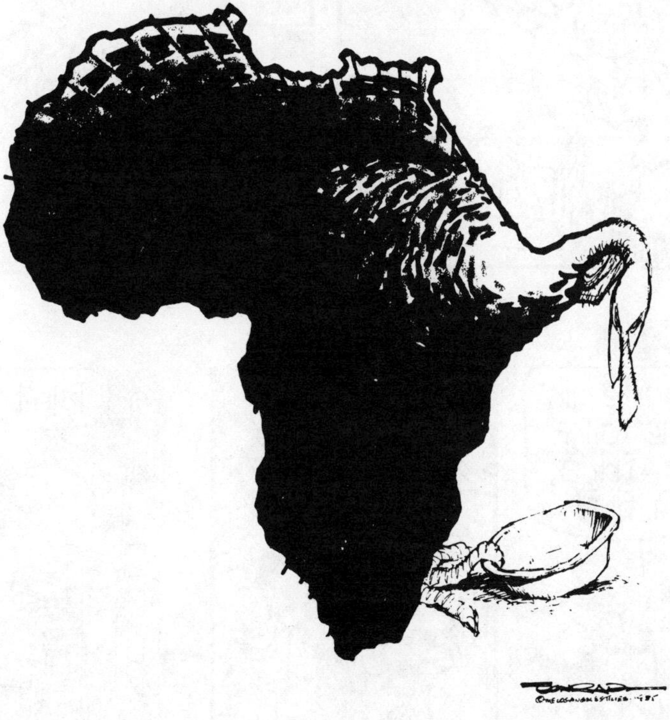
CONRAD

HÄGAR the Horrible ® by Dik Browne

WHAT ARE YOU DOING, DAD ?
I'M SHARING WITH THE HUNGRY OF THE WORLD
© 1985 King Features Syndicate, Inc. World rights reserved.
CAN A VIKING DO THAT ?
OF COURSE...
AFTER ALL, I'M NOT A BARBARIAN!
DIK BROWNE
11-28

GASOLINE ALLEY® *by Dick Moores*

What is we haulin' wher', Joel?
Food fer th' fine folks in Africa, Rufus!
Joe!
11/28
© 1985 Tribune Media Services, Inc. All Rights Reserved
Ain't Africa kinda' far?
Tain't close..
..but onc't we gits acros't th' ol' bridge it's a piece o' cake!
Dick Moores

2

MOON MULLINS ®

by Ferd and Tom Johnson

FOOD FOR THOUGHT...
TURKEY'S ON TH' TABLE, PROF! COM'ON-- WE'RE WAITIN' FOR YA!
SOON AS I FINISH WRITING THIS CHECK FOR THE WORLD HUNGER RELIEF PROGRAM, KAYO.
11 28
HURRY IT UP-- WE'RE STARVIN'!
© 1985 Tribune Media Services, Inc. All Rights Reserved
NO, LAD-- WE'RE NOT...
THAT'S WHY WE CALL IT THANKS-GIVING...
FERD + TOM JOHNSON

HOWIE ®

by Howie Schneider

SOMETIMES IT SEEMS THAT WHILE HALF THE WORLD IS STARVING, THE OTHER HALF IS OUT TO LUNCH
Schneider
11·28
© 1985 United Feature Syndicate, Inc.

DRABBLE® by Kevin Fagan

AS WE GIVE THANKS FOR THE FOOD ON OUR TABLE, LET'S REMEMBER THOSE WHO AREN'T AS FORTUNATE.
WHAT FOOD? I DON'T SEE ANY FOOD ON OUR TABLE!
THERE'S BEEN A SLIGHT DELAY, DAD...
11/28
NORMAN ACCIDENTALLY DROPPED THE TURKEY, AND THEN HE STEPPED ON IT.
SO NOW HE'S CLEANING IT OFF?
NO, HE'S TRYING TO GET HIS FOOT OUT OF IT!
FAGAN
© 1985 United Feature Syndicate, Inc.

ROBOTMAN T.M. by Jim Meddick

Hey, Oscar, all the comics today are about feeding needy people...
That's right. There are a lot of people on this planet who have no food.
You know... like no batteries...
© 1985 United Feature Syndicate, Inc.
Meddick 11-28
GET ME MY CHECK-BOOK!
Right away!

THE FAR SIDE By GARY LARSON

© 1985 Universal Press Syndicate
Larson
Lulu's
11-28

"Hey! Where's everybody going? *I* still have one or two empty stomachs."

ZIGGY® by Tom Wilson

... AND AS WE REACH FOR SECOND HELPINGS... PLEASE HELP ALL THOSE WHO ARE REACHING OUT FOR FIRSTS!
11-28
© 1985 Universal Press Syndicate
Tom Wilson

MOTLEY'S CREW

by Ben Templeton & Tom Forman

GEE, POP, CONSIDERING THE NUMBER OF HUNGRY PEOPLE IN THE WORLD, I DON'T THINK WE'RE DOING ENOUGH.
IT WOULD BE ENOUGH, TRUMAN...,
..IF EVERYBODY DID IT.
©1985 Tribune Media Services, Inc. All Rights Reserved
11/28

WRIGHT ANGLES®

by Larry Wright

THIS JUST CAME IN THE MAIL. IT'S A ONE-WAY TICKET TO AFRICA.
© 1985 United Feature Syndicate, Inc.
MUST BE A MISTAKE. WHY WOULD ANYONE IN MY FAMILY WANT A ONE-WAY TICKET TO AFRICA?
NO MISTAKE.
IF I'M GOING TO FILL SOMEONE'S BELLY, I'D RATHER IT BE SOMEONE WHO REALLY NEEDS IT.
11/28
LARRY WRIGHT

STEVE ROPER & MIKE NOMAD — BY SAUNDERS & MATERA

CAN I HAVE LUNCH BEFORE I GO TO MAIL MY LETTER, MA JONG?
IT'S ON THE TABLE, LON! ...SOMETHING SPECIAL FOR TODAY!
© News America Syndicate, 1985
RICE?!?
ENJOY!...AND CONSIDER THE MILLIONS WHO WOULD GIVE THANKS TO BE SO FORTUNATE!
MATERA and SAUNDERS 11-28

BABYMAN® — by Don Addis

I WISH I COULD SHARE THIS BOUNTY WITH THE TRULY HUNGRY PEOPLE OF THE WORLD!
11-28
ESPECIALLY THE STRAINED SPINACH, RIGHT?
don addis
NOBODY COULD BE THAT HUNGRY!
© 1985 by NEA, Inc.

THE FAMILY CIRCUS® By Bil Keane

11-28
BIL KEANE

"How 'bout if I eat just one more bite and we send the rest to Africa?"

TODAY'S WORLD

CHARLIE, LET'S DONATE THE CROP TO HELP WORLD HUNGER.
CAN'T, ZELDA. THE BANK JUST SEIZED THE FARM.
DAVID BROWN.
11-28

CAPTAIN VINCIBLE® By Ralph Smith

HOW LONG WILL IT TAKE ME TO GROW ENOUGH FOOD TO ELIMINATE WORLD HUNGER?
FOR YOU?! —I'D SAY ABOUT A ZILLION YEARS!
© 1985 King Features Syndicate, Inc. World rights reserved.
11-28
HOW ABOUT IF I WORK WEEKENDS?
SEED
SMITH

TIGER® By Bud Blake

DINNER READY, TIGER? I'M STARVING!
STARVING! YOU DON'T KNOW WHAT STARVING IS LIKE
© 1985 King Features Syndicate, Inc. World rights reserved.
NOBODY OUGHT TO KNOW WHAT STARVING IS LIKE
11-28
BUD BLAKE

STEVE CANYON

By Milton Caniff

11/28
© News America Syndicate U.S.A. 1985. Derechos Reservados Steve Canyon. Luis Ciclon
QUIZ, HURRY WITH THE TRANSMITTER!
SOME OF THESE INJURED WILL NOT LAST LONG WITH-OUT MEDICAL SUPPLIES!
I DON'T KNOW WHICH IS WORSE — SUDDEN KILLING IN AN EARTHQUAKE...
MILTON CANIFF
...OR THE LONG, SLOW DEATH OF HUNGRY PEOPLE EVERYWHERE!

Adam®

by Brian Basset

© 1985 Universal Press Syndicate
OK, WHO'S HUNGRY?
BOTH HANDS, CLAYTON? YOU MUST HAVE AN EXTRA-LARGE APPETITE.
BRIAN BASSET
11-28
NO.... SOME OF US AREN'T PRESENT.

cathy®

by Cathy Guisewite

FINISH UP THE TURKEY, CATHY. THERE ARE CHILDREN STARVING IN ETHIOPIA.
MY EATING TURKEY IS NOT GOING TO HELP CHILDREN IN ETHIOPIA, MOM!
FINISH THE BROCCOLI. THERE ARE CHILDREN STARVING IN BANGLADESH.
MY EATING BROCCOLI IS NOT GOING TO HELP CHILDREN IN BANGLADESH!!
FINISH THE PIE SMOTHERED IN FRESH, FLUFFY WHIPPED CREAM. THERE ARE CHILDREN STARVING IN HAITI.
OK.
WE ALL HAVE A POINT WHERE WE'RE COMPELLED TO GIVE.
GUISEWITE
11-28
© 1985 Universal Press Syndicate

BRINGING UP FATHER

by Frank Johnson

HERE'S YOUR PIZZA!
SHALL I CUT IT INTO SIX OR EIGHT SLICES!
BETTER MAKE IT SIX...
...I DON'T THINK I CAN EAT EIGHT SLICES!
FRANK JOHNSON
11-28
ON SECOND THOUGHT, BIMMY, KEEP ON CUTTING! GIVE TO USA FOR AFRICA

MARMADUKE® by Brad Anderson

11·28
© 1985 United Feature Syndicate,Inc
BRAD ANDERSON

"Marmaduke is sharing his Thanksgiving dinner!"

DUNAGIN'S PEOPLE

11-28
Dunagin
1985 The Orlando Sentinel
News America Syndicate

"LET'S DO LUNCH SOMETIME."

SALLY FORTH

BY GREG HOWARD

LOOK AT ALL THIS FOOD, MOM. I DON'T KNOW WHETHER TO FEEL THANKFUL FOR ALL WE HAVE OR GUILTY THAT OTHERS ARE HUNGRY.
I USUALLY FEEL BOTH, HONEY.
© News America Syndicate, 1985
I START THE MEAL BY GIVING THANKS. LATER, AS I STRUGGLE TO PUSH MY OVERSTUFFED BODY AWAY FROM THE TABLE, A WAVE OF GUILT SWEEPS OVER ME.
I ALWAYS THOUGHT THAT WAS INDIGESTION.
11-28
howard

AGATHA CRUMM®

By Bill Hoest

THERE YOU ARE EATING AGAIN, JUNIOR!
DON'T YOU EVER WORRY ABOUT ALL THE HUNGRY PEOPLE IN THE WORLD?
I DO, MOTHER. I WORRY SO MUCH I GET TENSE!
AND YOU KNOW WHAT HAPPENS WHEN I GET TENSE.
11-28 HOEST
WHAT?
I EAT!

Ellie by Ray Helle

DO YOU KNOW WHAT IT'S LIKE TO BE HUNGRY?
11/28
I MEAN, TO REALLY FEEL THE PANGS OF STARVATION..
©1985 RAY HELLE
TO BE SO WEAK YOU CAN HARDLY MOVE.
POOR SAM
RAY HELLE
THERE WERE NO TWINKIES FOR HIS MORNING SNACK.

GRUBBY By Warren Sattler

NOTHING COULD MAKE ME FEEL BETTER THAN TO SPEND MAH MONEY ON A GOURMET MEAL FOR MYSELF!
GIVE TO USA FOR AFRICA
©1985 BY AL SMITH FEATURE SERVICE
AH WAS WRONG!
USA for AFRICA
WARREN SATTLER
WON'T YOU GIVE TOO?
11-28-85

CALDWELL

© 1985 King Features Syndicate, Inc. World rights reserved.
CALDWELL
11-28

"MORNING, MA'AM. I REPRESENT A WELL-MEANING YET MISGUIDED CIVIC GROUP. TODAY WE'RE ASKING FOLKS TO DONATE A COOKBOOK TO THE HUNGRY."

HAZEL

ICE CREAM
© 1985 King Features Syndicate, Inc. World rights reserved.

"We're so lucky. Think of the millions who are going to bed hungry tonight."

Ted Key
FROM:
TO:
ICE CREAM
11-28

"Thoughtful, hon. But instead of ice cream, why don't we send..."

BEETLE BAILEY® — By Mort Walker

HERE WE ARE ABOUT TO SIT DOWN TO A BIG THANKS-GIVING DINNER AND PEOPLE ARE STILL STARVING IN AFRICA
I WISH WE COULD SEND THEM OUR TURKEY
11-28
©1985 King Features Syndicate, Inc. World rights reserved.
POST OFFICE
OF COURSE WE MEANT IT, BUT...
MORT WALKER

ROSE IS ROSE ® — by Pat Brady

GO AHEAD, PASQUALE!
MMMM! T'ANK YOO!
©1985 United Feature Syndicate, Inc.
11-28
HE SAYS A SIMPLE BUT SINCERE GRACE!

DEAR LORD, WE THANK YOU FOR THIS FEAST, AND WE THANK YOU THAT WE ARE NOT HUNGRY...
LIKE THEY ARE IN AFRICA.
AUTH
11/28/85. THE PHILADELPHIA INQUIRER, UNIVERSAL PRESS SYNDICATE

NANCY®

by Jerry Scott

DINNER IS ALMOST READY, NANCY
GREAT! I'M STARVING!
© 1985 United Feature Syndicate, Inc.
PAT PAT
...RELATIVELY SPEAKING
JERRY SCOTT
11-28

ALLEY OOP ®

by Dave Graue

HOW COME BUBBA ISN'T EATING?
BECAUSE THERE ARE THE "HAVES", AN' TH' "HAVE NOTS" IN THIS WORLD, OOP!
CHOMP CHOMP
11-28
...AN' TH' "HAVES" ALWAYS RE-MEMBER TO BRING SOME FOOD WITH 'EM!
WHAT IF THEY DON'T HAVE ANY FOOD TO BRING IN TH' FIRST PLACE?
© 1985 by NEA, Inc
WELL, I, UH....
HERE, BUBBA, I'LL SHARE MINE WITH YOU! NOBODY OUGHTA GO HUNGRY!
GEE, THANKS, OOP!
FOR SOME REASON, I JUST LOST MY APPETITE!
THEN YOU WON'T OBJECT IF I EAT YOUR LEFTOVERS!
GRAUE 11-28

B.C.

BY JOHNNY HART

WE'RE STARVING, ... WHERE'S THE THANKSGIVING TURKEY ?
I SET HIM FREE !
YOU WHAT ?
AS LONG AS ONE HUMAN AMONG US MUST GO WITHOUT FOOD... THEN SHALL ALL HUMANS GO WITHOUT FOOD !
WHAT ABOUT US TURKEYS ?... YOU FAT FREAK !
© News America Syndicate, 1985
11·28
hart

CHEEVERWOOD

by Michael Fry

WHAT A THANKSGIVING! MY SAAB BREAKS DOWN... I MISS MY FLIGHT TO CLUB MED... AND NOW I'M STUCK IN THIS STUPID BAR WATCHING T.V.
Cafe PHIL
WHAT DO I HAVE TO BE THANKFUL FOR?!...
...IN OTHER NEWS THIS THANKSGIVING, FAMINE VICTIMS IN AFRICA WERE ASKED WHAT THEY WERE MOST THANKFUL FOR. THE ANSWER FOR MANY...
..."HOPE."
WHERE'D SHE GO?
EMERGENCY FOOTENDECTOMY.
11/28
©1985, Washington Post Writers Group
Michael Fry

MC GONIGLE OF THE CHRONICLE

BY JEFF DANZIGER

THAT'S WHY THANKSGIVING IS THE MOST DIFFICULT HOLIDAY...
WHY?
11-28
CAUSE, YOU HAVE TO BE THANKFUL THAT YOU HAVE SO MUCH... BUT YOU ALSO KNOW THAT OTHER PEOPLE HAVE SO LITTLE...
© News America Syndicate, 1985
LOOKIT!! CUT IT OUT! ALL I WANNA DO IS ENJOY MY TURKEY! NOT FEEL GUILTY!
Chronicle
GEE... I'M SORRY, FITZ... I DIDN'T MEAN TO MAKE YOU FEEL GUILTY...
HONEST I DINT...
HOOMPH!!
DANZIGER

SYDNEY T.M.

by Scott Stantis

...SO MANY HUNGRY PEOPLE... I HAVE A LOT TO BE THANKFUL FOR...
11-28
STANTIS
...BUT THE THING I'M MOST THANKFUL FOR IS...
© 1985 United Feature Syndicate, Inc.
...I'M AT THE TOP OF THE FOOD CHAIN!

my grandma...
© 1985 King Features Syndicate, Inc. World rights reserved.
11-28
DONNA SOTT
...would feed the whole world if she had enough chairs.

BIZARRO BY DAN PIRARO

TICKETS
© Chronicle Features, 1985
PIRARO
AB
AIRLINES

"TWO TICKETS TO THE THIRD WORLD, PLEASE"...

POPEYE® **By Bud Sagendorf**

YER FAT AN' DISGUSTIPATIN'!
I AM HUNGRY, SIR!
© 1985 King Features Syndicate, Inc. World rights reserved.
YOU EATS MORE THAN YOUR SHARE OF FOODS!
11/28
BUD SAGENDORF
DOES YOU REALIZE 'AT ONLY FIVE PERCENT OF WHAT YOU PUTS IN THERE COULD FEED A THOUSING STARVIN' LI'L KIDS?
?
?

THE CRASS MENAGERIE by Kyle Baker

YOU KNOW, I SENT SOME MONEY TO HELP THE STARVING, BUT I SUSPECT I JUST DID IT TO KEEP FROM FEELING GUILTY.
DO YOU SUPPOSE IT'S POSSIBLE TO DO THE RIGHT THING FOR THE WRONG REASON, FERD?
WELL, ART, IT'S, UH...
11-28
UH, YOU KNOW WHAT THEY SAY... UH... WAITAMINUTE... HEY, CHARLIE, ISN'T THERE AN OLD SAYING FOR THIS?
"ANY PORT IN A STORM"?
THANKS, CHARLIE.
"IT'S NOT THE THOUGHT, IT'S THE PRESENT THAT COUNTS".
SHUT UP.
© 1985 BAKER

WILLY 'N ETHEL BY JOE MARTIN

©News America Syndicate, 1985
JOE MARTIN
11-28

"BOY, ETHEL, THESE BIRDS ARE REALLY MAKING ME HUNGRY!"

LEOTOONS
© LEONARD BRUCE CHARLES DURCK
WE CARTOON CHARACTERS HAVE ONE THING OVER HUMANS. WE DON'T HAVE TO EAT!
SUPPORT USA FOR AFRICA

BONER'S ARK

by Frank Johnson

I GAVE MORE BECAUSE I DIETED THE LONGEST!
YOU ALSO ATE THE MOST TO BEGIN WITH!...
NO! I GAVE THE MOST BECAUSE I ATE THE LEAST!
I DID!
NO, I DID!
NO, I DID!
SPLASH!
HAPPY THANKSGIVING!
USA for AFRICA
FRANK JOHNSON 11-28
©1985, KING FEATURES SYNDICATE, INC.

TIM TYLER'S LUCK®

By Bob Young

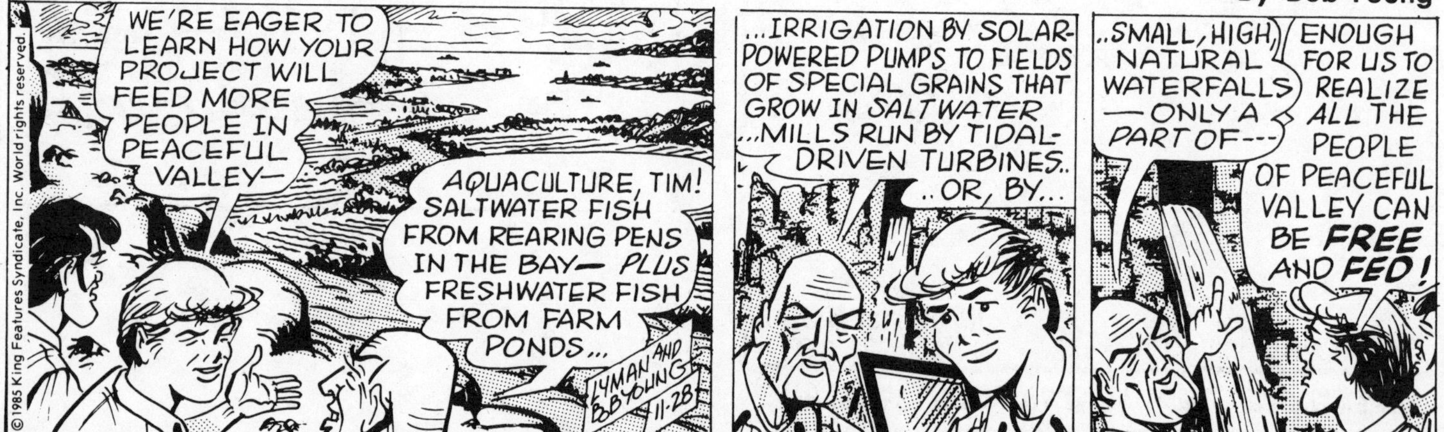
WE'RE EAGER TO LEARN HOW YOUR PROJECT WILL FEED MORE PEOPLE IN PEACEFUL VALLEY—
AQUACULTURE, TIM! SALTWATER FISH FROM REARING PENS IN THE BAY— PLUS FRESHWATER FISH FROM FARM PONDS...
LYMAN AND BOB YOUNG 11-28
©1985 King Features Syndicate, Inc. World rights reserved.
...IRRIGATION BY SOLAR-POWERED PUMPS TO FIELDS OF SPECIAL GRAINS THAT GROW IN SALTWATER ...MILLS RUN BY TIDAL-DRIVEN TURBINES.. ..OR, BY...
..SMALL, HIGH, NATURAL WATERFALLS — ONLY A PART OF---
ENOUGH FOR US TO REALIZE ALL THE PEOPLE OF PEACEFUL VALLEY CAN BE FREE AND FED!

BENCHLEY™ — By Dumas and Drucker

WE'VE GIVEN AWAY MILLIONS AND MILLIONS TO STARVING NATIONS...
HOW COME THE RUSSIANS HAVE DONE SO LITTLE?
11-28
WELL, THEY DID MAKE A LARGE OFFER OF FOOD TO CERTAIN COUNTRIES, BUT IT WAS REJECTED.
Copyright 1985 Cowles Syndicate Inc.
WHY?
THEY WANTED TO USE TANKS TO MAKE THE DELIVERIES.

ASK SHAGG® — by Peter Guren

Dear Mouth,
What is a baby turkey called?
KARA
FT. COLLINS, CO
FREE SHAGG DOLL IF WE USE YOUR QUESTION ABOUT ANIMALS! SEND TO "ASK SHAGG" c/o THIS NEWSPAPER.
A BABY TURKEY IS CALLED A "POULT."
GOO-GOO
MA MA?
(c) 1985 United Feature Syndicate, Inc.
AFTER 2 TO 3 DAYS IT'S CALLED A "YOUNG TURKEY" AND AFTER 3 TO 4 WEEKS IT'S CALLED A "TURKEY"...
...AND AFTER 24 TO 26 WEEKS IT'S CALLED A "THANKSGIVING DINNER."
THERE MUST BE A BETTER WAY TO DONATE TO THE CAUSE OF HUNGER.
GUREN

HERMAN®

by Jim Unger

11/28
© 1985 Universal Press Syndicate

"Have you ever thought about sending your lunch to an African village?"

BROTHER JUNIPER

by Fred McCarthy

PRAYER KNOCKS...
FASTING OBTAINS...
MERCY RECEIVES...
HELP the STARVING in AFRICA...TODAY!
© News America Syndicate, 1985
11·28

ARLO AND JANIS™ by Jimmy Johnson

GENE! WITH ALL THE HUNGRY PEOPLE IN THE WORLD, YOU'RE NOT GOING TO LEAVE ALL THAT FOOD!
AW, MOM...
GLUTTONY SURE IS A STRANGE WAY TO EXPRESS CONCERN FOR THE STARVING!
JOHNSON
IT SEEMS TO ME IF THERE'S BLAME HERE, IT'S THE COOK'S--FOR PREPARING FAR MORE THAN THREE CAN EAT...
11/28
© 1985 by NEA, Inc.
BUT I WASN'T GOING TO SAY ANYTHING!

CAPTAIN EASY® by Crooks & Casale

SOME THANKSGIVING, EH, EASY?
IT COULD BE WORSE... AT LEAST WE'RE NOT HUNGRY...
HEY, PAL, YA GOT A SMOKE?
?
CROOKS & CASALE 11-28
UH, A SMOKE?
YOU KNOW, A CIGARETTE.
© 1985 by NEA, Inc
YA WANNA SMOKE?
READY?

CROCK

by Bill Rechin & Don Wilder

©News America Syndicate, 1985
DID YOU ENJOY THE THANKSGIVING CRUMB I GAVE YOU, FIGOWITZ?
I SENT IT TO THE HUNGRY PEOPLE IN AFRICA
WHAT THE HECK, PEANUT BUTTER AND CRANBERRY SAUCE AIN'T SO BAD
TO AFRICA
11·28
Rechin & WILDER

MR. MEN™ AND LITTLE MISS™

by Hargreaves & Sellers

© 1985 Hargreaves and Sellers
Distributed by NEA, Inc
11-28
Sellers

SHOE

by Jeff MacNelly

HOW WAS THAT THANKSGIVING DINNER?...
GREAT, ROZ!... AND I'M THANKFUL FOR EACH AND EVERY (BURP) MORSEL IN MY ACHING TUMMY.
YOU OUGHTA BE THANKFUL FOR WHAT'S NOT IN THERE.
AND WHAT COULD THAT POSSIBLY BE?
HUNGER PAINS.
MACNELLY
© Jefferson Communications, Inc. 1985
Distributed by Tribune Media Services, Inc.

Annie

by Leonard Starr

...NO USE TRYIN' T'CLIMB BACK UP THROUGH THAT HOLE, SANDY... I KEEP SLIPPIN' BACK...
...BUT SINCE AMITY PULLS HER VANISHING ACT BY WAY O' THIS TUNNEL, THERE'S GOT T' BE A WAY OUT O' HERE!
LEONARD STARR
11-26
IS THIS WIND... TRYING TO KEEP US FROM REACHING THE DODSON HOUSE, PUNJAB?
NO... IT SEEMS TO BE PUSHING US TOWARD IT... SAHIB!...

THE LEE WAY

COULD YOU PLEASE END WORLD HUNGER..
OKAY, I'LL DO IT!
I DON'T BELIEVE IT. IT WAS TOO EASY.
Bill Lee

GINO by gene machamer

© MAC
GENE MACHAMER

"For our school's food drive, I'll need our carrots, broccoli, liver, and. . ."

SNAKE TALES™

by Sols

OH, GREAT SPIRIT, WHAT LIES IN THE FUTURE?
©SALISBURY-1985 Distributed by NEA, Inc.
SHELTER FOR THE HOMELESS. FOOD FOR THE STARVING AND EQUALITY FOR ALL MANKIND!!
11-28
WOW!
ARE THINGS GOING TO BE THAT GOOD?
THEY'RE THE LIES, YOU DIM-WIT!!
SOLS

MR. ABERNATHY®

By Frank Ridgeway

YOU'RE LATE AGAIN, PIERRE!!
YAWN
YOU'RE NOT KEEPING UP TO YOUR RESPONSIBILITY!
11-28
YOU FORGOT MY BREAKFAST TOO!!
CRUNCHOS
FRANK RIDGEWAY

MISS PEACH

by Mell Lazarus

ENJOY YOUR THANKSGIVING DINNER, ARTHUR?
YES. I'M STUFFED!
THERE ARE KIDS, MILLIONS OF THEM, WHO HAVE NEVER SEEN THAT MUCH FOOD IN THEIR LIVES.
TRUE. GEE, WE'RE LUCKY, AREN'T WE?
YES, WE ARE. FROM NOW ON, LET'S TRY TO SPREAD SOME OF THAT LUCK AROUND. OKAY?
© News America Syndicate, 1985
MELL LAZARUS
11-28

EEK & MEEK ®

by Howie Schneider

MONIQUE'S MEALS
TODAY
AFRICAN FOOD
© 1985 by NEA, Inc.
11·28
IT MEANS SHE'S CLOSED!

LUTHER

By Brumsic Brandon, Jr.

MARY FRANCES, WHAT DOES YOUR TRIVIA BOOK SAY ABOUT HUNGER?
I'LL LOOK IT UP FOR YOU, PEE WEE!
©1985 Los Angeles Times Syndicate
11-28
IT SAYS "THERE IS NOTHING TRIVIAL ABOUT HUNGER!"
BRANDON JR

FLASH GORDON®

By Dan Barry

IT'S SHEER *INSANITY*! NOW MING—AT WAR WITH HIS ALLIES, THE LIZARDMEN!
I UNDERSTAND THE LIZARDMEN STRUCK FIRST!
BARRY & FUJITANI 11-28
END WORLD HUNGER.
THEN MING IS THE *VICTIM* OF THE SAME HOSTILITIES AS OUR ALLIES!
THAT COULD MEAN...
...THAT MING IS *NOT* THE TROUBLEMAKER, BARIN! WHO, THEN?
© 1985 King Features Syndicate, Inc. World rights reserved.

BELVEDERE BY CRENSHAW

©News America Syndicate, 1985
GEORGE CRENSHAW
11-28

" MAYBE WE'D BETTER JUST OPEN A COUPLE OF TV DINNERS AND LET IT GO AT THAT. "

OFF THE LEASH™ by W.B. Park

HUNGER IS A TERRIBLE THING ~ ESPECIALLY AROUND DINNERTIME!
© 1985 United Feature Syndicate, Inc.
Park 11-28

SYLVIA **by Nicole Hollander**

Disturbing Dreams
© 1985 by Nicole Hollander
I DREAMT I ASKED THE PRESIDENT IF HE WOULD SKIP THANKSGIVING DINNER AND SEND THE MONEY TO STARVING PEOPLE IN AFRICA, BUT HE SAID HE COULDN'T DO THAT BECAUSE IT WOULDN'T BE FAIR TO THE STARVING PEOPLE IN AMERICA.
11-28
Nicole Hollander

the small society **by Brickman**

© 1985 King Features Syndicate, Inc. World rights reserved.
SURE, I'LL SEND ANOTHER CHECK TO U.S.A. FOR AFRICA...
BUT I'D BETTER HANG UP NOW — THE TURKEY AND MY WIFE ARE GETTING COLD!
11-28
BRICKMAN — Yates

WINSTON

BY BURNETT & SAJEM

MAIL THIS!
$1
'TO U.S.A. FOR AFRICA'— WHERE'D YOU GET ALL THAT MONEY, WINSTON?
BURNETT & SAJEM
YOU MISSED THE GARAGE SALE!
© News America Syndicate, 1985
11-28

HUBERT®

By Dick Wingert

HUBERT! FOR HEAVEN'S SAKE— DINNER!
© 1985 King Features Syndicate, Inc. World rights reserved.
Wingert
AREN'T YOU HUNGRY?
NOT QUITE
NOW I AM!
I'VE WRITTEN OUR CHECK FOR THOSE LESS FORTUNATE
11-28

36

PAVLOV® by Ted Martin

$1
BUY A CHOCOLATE CHIP COOKIE
Proceeds to the FAMINE RELIEF FUND
TedMartin
© 1985 Universal Press Syndicate
11-28

"I bought a cookie, and now he tells me I've got to donate it to a charity of his choice."

Berry's World

11-28 © 1985 by NEA. Inc

ON THE FASTRACK®

By Bill Holbrook

BOB, THE TRICK TO PHILANTHROPY IS TO EMPATHIZE WITH PEOPLE IN DISTRESS!
SO WHEN I DECIDED TO HELP IN THE FIGHT AGAINST WORLD HUNGER, I MADE A CONTRIBUTION THAT SHOWED, DESPITE OUR CULTURAL DIFFERENCES, THAT I UNDERSTOOD THEIR BASIC NEEDS!
WHAT'D YOU SEND?
WHO THE HECK SENT A SHIPMENT OF "WE ARE THE WORLD" ALBUMS?
RED CROSS
Bill Holbrook
11/28
© 1985 King Features Syndicate, Inc. World rights reserved.

ELWOOD

by Ben Templeton & Tom Forman

Today some people on earth will give thanks for the food on their tables...
..let us hope a day dawns soon where all people on earth can give thanks for the food on their tables~
Elwood
11/28
© 1985 Tribune Media Services, Inc. All Rights Reserved

JOHN DARLING

BY BATIUK & SHAMRAY

OH...
WHAT DID AL WANT?
HE HEARD THAT WE WERE DEVOTING OUR SHOW TODAY TO THE SUBJECT OF HUNGER...
AND HE THOUGHT IT WAS A FEATURE ON THE FLOOR CREW!
© News America Syndicate, 1985
11-28 BATIUK/SHAMRAY

BUZ SAWYER®

By John Celardo

PLEASE, I HAVE A SURPRISE FOR YOU... COME!
HEY, BUZ— THIS MIGHT BE A TRAP!
END WORLD HUNGER.
WHAT HAPPENED TO THE GUYS WHO WERE TRYING TO ROAST ME?
I THINK I'VE WORKED A MIRACLE WITH THEM!
© 1985 King Features Syndicate, Inc. World rights reserved.
11-28 JOHN CELARDO

HENRY® By Dick Hodgins

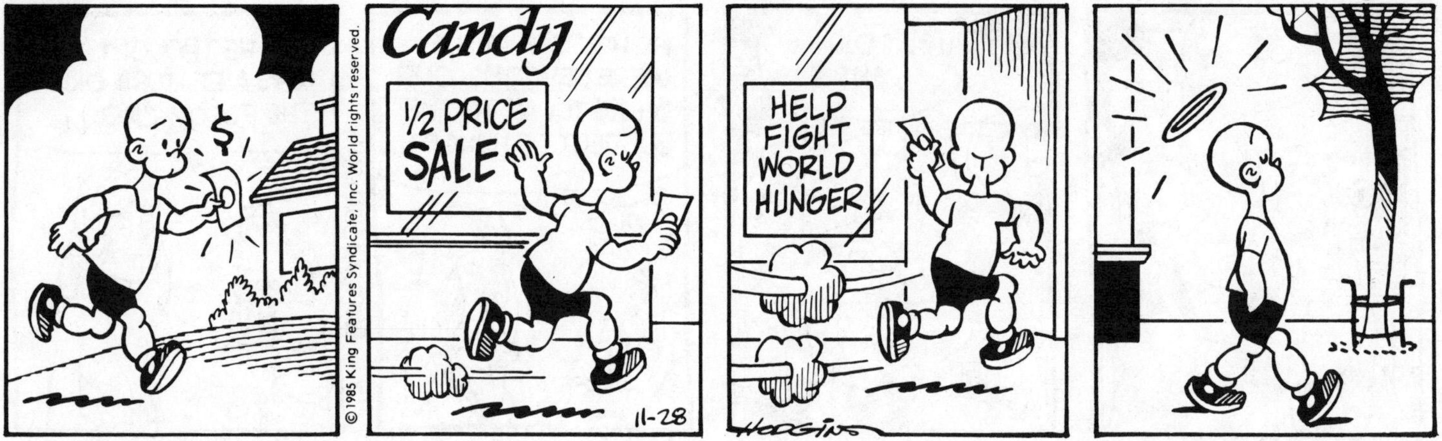

$
Candy
1/2 PRICE SALE
© 1985 King Features Syndicate, Inc. World rights reserved.
11-28
HELP FIGHT WORLD HUNGER
HODGINS

STOCKWORTH by Sterling and Selesnick

COLLECTING FOR WORLD HUNGER...
USA AFRIK
11 28
I CREATE JOBS!
IN ETHIOPIA?
© 1986 Sterling & Selesnick, Inc.
IT'S TAX DEDUCTIBLE
Sterling + Selesnick

Grimsly

by Harley Schwadron

SCHWADRON
HELP
© 1985 Harley Schwadron
Distributed by Extra Newspaper Features
11/28

"NO, I'M NOT ANOREXIC. I'M STARVING."

WINETOONS

by Robert Platt

HUNGER...
Let's
CRUSH
it out
everywhere...
Platt
©1985 ROBERT PLATT

...Pero Pa' Lante!

by Harold Jessurun

MAMi...¿YA ESTÁ EL PAVO?
YA MiSMO.
© 1985 por Harold Jessurun
¡AVANZA MAMi QUE ME ESTOY MURIENDO DE HAMBRE!
JESSURUN
NO SABEN LO AFORTUNADOS QUE SON PORQUE TIENEN QUÉ COMER EN ESTE DÍA DE ACCIÓN DE GRACIAS. AHORA MISMO HAY MILLONES DE PERSONAS MURIÉNDOSE DE HAMBRE. TÚ LOS PUEDES AYUDAR DONANDO LO QUE PUEDAS. BUSCA EL CUPÓN DE AYUDA EN EL PERIÓDICO DE HOY Y..... ¡¡ENVUÉLVETE!!

FUNKY WINKERBEAN

BY TOM BATIUK

WHEN PEOPLE FOUND OUT THAT WE WERE DONATING ALL THE FUNDS FROM OUR TURKEY SALES TO HELP ELIMINATE WORLD HUNGER... THEY SOLD LIKE HOTCAKES!
© News America Syndicate 1985
WAIT A SECOND ... THAT'S IT! BAND HOTCAKES!!
WHY, I'LL BET WE COULD SELL ...
HARRY! SIT DOWN AND EAT YOUR TURKEY!
BATIUK
11-28

COOPER®

by Mike Keefe and Tim Menees

CLASS, YOU RAISED A GOOD POINT ABOUT THE INEQUITIES IN THE WORLD'S FOOD SUPPLY AND THE BROTHERHOOD OF MAN!
VAN BUREN
Keefe MENEES
WHAT THEN SHOULD WE REALLY BE THINKING ABOUT THIS THANKSGIVING?
11·28
ST. LOUIS AT DALLAS!
© 1985 Universal Press Syndicate

DOCTOR SMOCK ®

by George Lemont

COMBAT HUNGER! MAKE A DONATION TODAY! TO: USA FOR AFRICA!
GEE, HAVING THAT SIGN ON YOUR WALL SHOWS ME YOU ARE A KIND AND COMPASSIONATE HUMAN BEING, DOCTOR!
WAIT'LL SHE FINDS THIS TURKEY IS GONNA BILL HER DOUBLE FOR HAVING TO WORK ON A HOLIDAY!
© 1985 United Feature Syndicate, Inc.
11-28
LEMONT

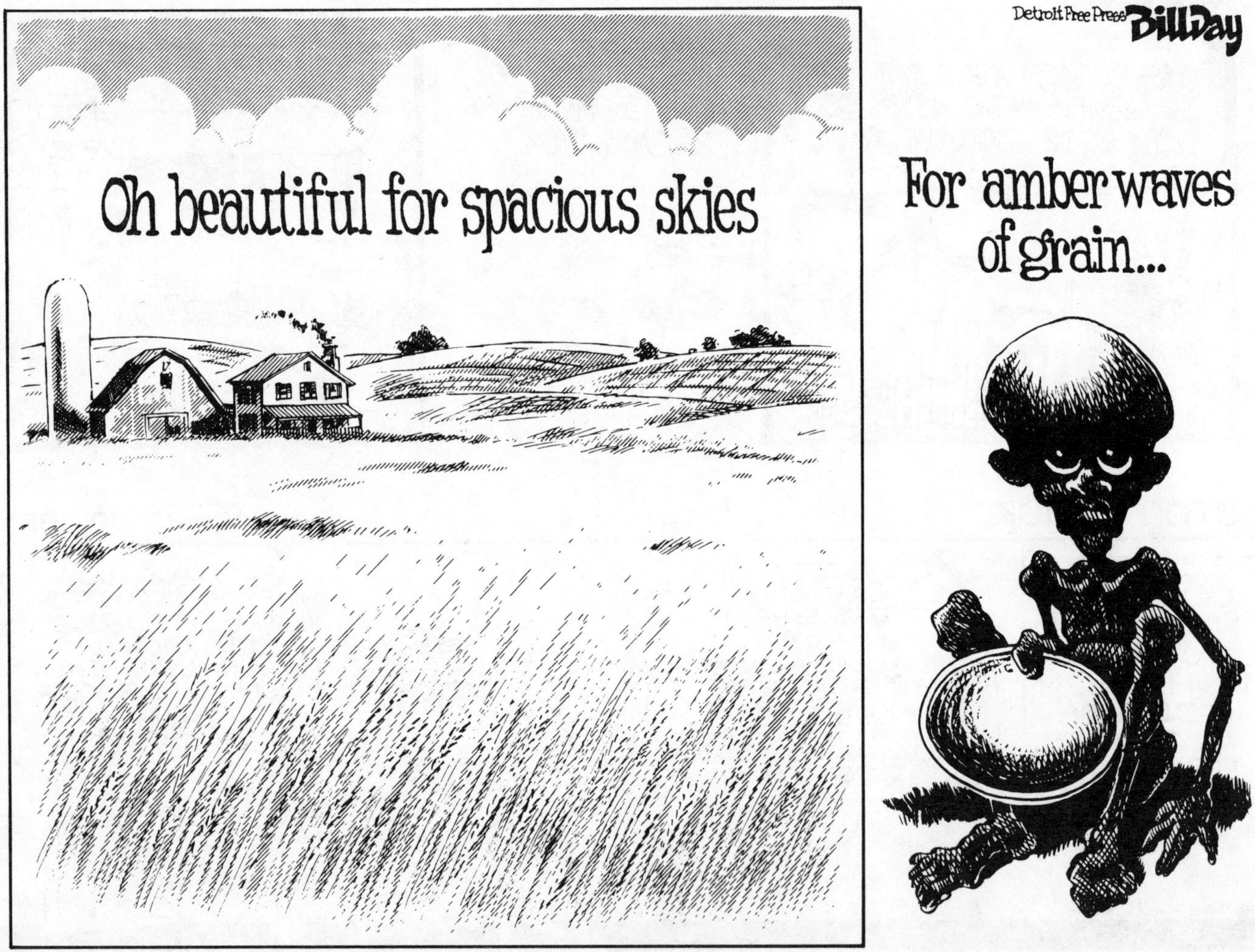
Detroit Free Press Bill Day
Oh beautiful for spacious skies
For amber waves of grain...

MILES TO GO

BY PHIL FRANK

.. We have all been witness to the hunger present in the world around us this year.. ...so we should be especially thankful for the food we are blessed with..
11-28
© News America Syndicate, 1985
..We should also resolve in the future to not just talk about hunger but to do something about it. Amen.
Amen.
Amen.
Phil Frank
WELL.. IT WAS AN AWFULLY BIG TURKEY.

EXECUTIVE SUITE™

by William Wells & Jack Lindstrom

MR. STONE, I REALLY NEED A RAISE.
© 1985 United Feature Syndicate, Inc.
DO YOU REALIZE YOUR PRESENT SALARY IS EQUAL TO THE GROSS NATIONAL PRODUCT OF SOME AFRICAN NATIONS?
LINDSTROM/Wells
THAT'S WHY THEY'RE STARVING!
11-28

BRENDA STARR®

By Ramona Fradon
and Mary Schmich

BEFORE WE EAT, LET'S TAKE A MOMENT TO REFLECT ON WHAT EACH OF US MIGHT DO TO HELP THE HUNGRY AROUND THE WORLD.
I SAY WE NEED BETTER NEWS COVERAGE OF THE PROBLEM!
WHAT A GAL! BRENDA'S A GREAT WRITER AND SHE CAN COOK, TOO!
I'LL BET SHE HAD IT CATERED!
84
11·28
© 1985 Tribune Media Services, Inc. All Rights Reserved
FRADON and SCHMICH

The Underground Surrealists

Mick Cusimano

POETS DINE ON CHEESEBURGERS WHILE YUPPIES EAT LOBSTER.
R.U OUTAVIT
PULLET SURPRISE
R.U. OUTAVIT
© 1985 Mick Cusimano . . . Underground Surrealist Studios
BUT FOR SOME A CHEESEBURGER WOULD BE A FEAST.
LET'S LEND A HAND TO FILL THEIR CUPS.....
...WITH HOPE.

LAUGH TIME

Bob Schwete

"Be thankful for leftovers — after all, the world's hungry never have anything to have leftovers from!"

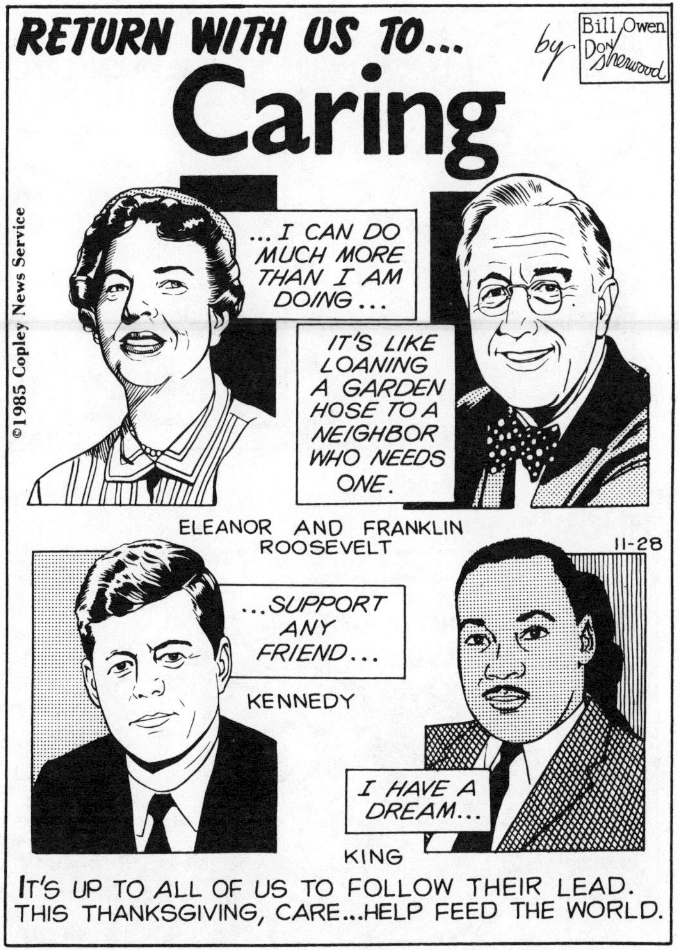
RETURN WITH US TO...
by Bill Owen Don Sherwood
Caring
©1985 Copley News Service
...I CAN DO MUCH MORE THAN I AM DOING...
IT'S LIKE LOANING A GARDEN HOSE TO A NEIGHBOR WHO NEEDS ONE.
ELEANOR AND FRANKLIN ROOSEVELT
11-28
...SUPPORT ANY FRIEND...
KENNEDY
I HAVE A DREAM...
KING
IT'S UP TO ALL OF US TO FOLLOW THEIR LEAD. THIS THANKSGIVING, CARE...HELP FEED THE WORLD.

Calvin and Hobbes

by Bill Watterson

THIS SMELLS LIKE BAT BARF!
THAT DOES IT, YOUNG MAN! YOU ARE EXCUSED TO YOUR ROOM!
DON'T YOU THINK THAT'S A LITTLE HARSH, DEAR? HE'LL GET HUNGRY.
CALVIN HAS GOT TO LEARN SOME MANNERS! HE WON'T STARVE TO DEATH.
...AND EXTRA PEPPERONI!
© 1985 Universal Press Syndicate
11-28
WATTERSON

RUDY™

by William Overgard

AS EATERS WE SHOULD THINK ABOUT THOSE WHO AREN'T EATING ON THANKSGIVING.
AND AS ANIMALS WE SHOULD GIVE THANKS THAT WE'RE NOT AMONG THOSE BEING EATEN.
© 1985 United Feature Syndicate, Inc.
OVERGARD 1985
11/28
PHARM

PEANUTS® by Charles M. Schulz

ARE YOU GOING TO HAVE A BIG THANKSGIVING DINNER, CHARLIE BROWN?
I SUPPOSE SO.. BIG DINNERS DON'T REALLY INTEREST ME...
I'VE NEVER THOUGHT THAT MUCH ABOUT EATING...
YOU DO WHEN YOUR DISH IS EMPTY!
SCHULZ
11-28
© 1985 United Feature Syndicate, Inc.

FERD'NAND® by Dahl Mikkelsen

DELICATESS
11-28
DELIC
© 1985 United Feature Syndicate, Inc.
AL

THE QUIGMANS by Buddy Hickerson

© 1985 Los Angeles Times Syndicate
11-28

"Ethiopia returned the parcel you sent. They didn't think coupons would do the trick."

PONYTAIL by Lee Holley

BIG BURGERS
11-28
LEE HOLLEY
© 1985 King Features Syndicate, Inc. World rights reserved.

"I'm glad we decided not to stop and eat and instead to think about the children in Africa who don't have such a choice!"

DICK TRACY®

By Dick Locher & Max Collins

WE HAVE STILL OTHER THINGS TO THINK ABOUT NOW.
WE HAVE TO ASSIST USA FOR AFRICA IN ENDING STARVATION— THAT'S ANOTHER CRIME WE NEED TO BE CONCERNED ABOUT...
DICK LOCHER MAX COLLINS
NOT TO MENTION QUIVER- A TERRORIST WHO WAGES WAR ON CAPITALISTS LIKE LABOCHE!
11 28
"I THINK WE KNOW WHAT THEY HAVE IN COMMON," TRACY SAYS.

MOOSE MILLER®

By Bob Weber

PLEASE, FOLKS, DON'T FORGET— THE STARVING PEOPLE OF AFRICA STILL NEED YOUR HELP
11-28
BOBWEBER

BLOOM COUNTY
by Berke Breathed

I'M COMING! I'M COMING! STOP YELLING!
© 1985 Washington Post Co.
AWRIGHT... NOW PLEASE TRY TO CONTROL YOURSELVES. THERE'S ENOUGH FOR EVERYONE... A LITTLE DIGNITY, PLEASE...
NOW STOP IT! STOP THAT PUSHING! AND ELBOWS OFF THE TABLE!!
FEEDING THE COCKROACHES A TURKEY DINNER FALLS FAR SHORT OF SOOTHING A GUILTY SOCIAL CONSCIENCE.
PASS THE GIBLETS!

ANIMAL CRACKERS®
by Roger Bollen

I WANT ALL OF YOU TO DO EVERYTHING YOU CAN TO END HUNGER IN THE WORLD!
WHO ARE YOU TALKING TO?
THE COMICS PAGE READERS!
I DECIDED TO GO RIGHT TO THE TOP!
11/28

The Peter Principle™ by Peter & Wuerker

Peter's Authority Principle: Everyone's wrong part of the time, but some of us exceed our time limit.
Dog Times
"NO HUNGER IN AMERICA" -WHITE HOUSE
11/28 © 1985 United Feature Syndicate, Inc.

GOOD NEWS • BAD NEWS by Henry Martin

© 1985 Tribune Media Services, Inc.
All Rights Reserved

"Dear Lord, we wish everybody in the whole world would have plenty to eat of everything. Except maybe okra and rhubarb."

Jim Henson's™ MUPPETS

by Guy and Brad Gilchrist

UNCLE KERMIT, CAN I HAVE A POSTAGE STAMP?
WHY, ROBIN?
I WANT TO SEND MY THANKSGIVING DAY DINNER TO SOMEONE WHO NEEDS IT MORE THAN ME!
©1986 KING FEATURES SYNDICATE, INC. WORLD RIGHTS RESERVED
IF THE CHILDREN ARE OUR FUTURE, THEN THE WORLD IS IN GOOD HANDS
GUY & BRAD GILCHRIST
11-28

Downstown®

by Tim Downs

SO A BUNCH OF US ROCK STARS GOT TOGETHER AND MADE AN ALBUM! AT OUR OWN EXPENSE!
THEN WE SOLD THE ALBUMS AND SENT ALL THE PROFITS TO YOU GUYS IN ETHIOPIA!
DID IT MAKE MUCH MONEY?
11·28
MUCH MONEY?!... HA! ALMOST AS MUCH AS WE MAKE IN A WHOLE YEAR!!
WE PAID OUR OWN CAB FARE AND EVERYTHING.
TIMDOWNS

ARNOLD **BY KEVIN MC CORMICK**

AND SO, THE INDIANS TAUGHT THE PILGRIMS HOW TO PLANT CROPS. AND THUS THEY WERE SAVED FROM STARVATION.
© News America Syndicate, 1985
THEY THEN JOINED TOGETHER TO THANK GOD FOR PROVIDING THE MEANS TO SUSTAIN LIFE.
AND THEY SHARED THEIR BLESSINGS AMONG ONE ANOTHER
WE'RE GOING TO EAT A BIRD.
HOLIDAYS CAN BE SO TRAUMATIC.
11/28

TWITCH **By How Rands**

COME ON, LUDWIG... LET'S MAKE IT A REAL THANKSGIVING DAY FOR THE CHILDERN
11-28
Al Smith Feature Service 1985

VIDIOTS — K. BOWSER

K. BOWSER
11·28
© 1985 Tribune Media Services, Inc
All Rights Reserved

"YOU SHOULD BE THANKFUL... THERE'S KIDS IN THIS WORLD THAT ONLY HAVE ONE SACK OF HALLOWEEN CANDY LEFT."

IT'S JUST A GAME™ — By Ed Morgan, Jr.

71
WORLD
HUNGER
11/28
Copyright 1985 Cowles Syndicate Inc.

Much more than a game.

FENTON

by Wiley

DO OTHER COUNTRIES HAVE A THANKSGIVING DAY?
THE PEOPLE OF ETHIOPIA CELEBRATE THANKSGIVING
WHEN DO THEY HAVE IT?
ANY DAY THEY CAN GET SOMETHING TO EAT
©NEWS AMERICA SYNDICATE 1985
11-28

WEE PALS

BY MORRIE TURNER

HOW WAS YOUR *THANKSGIVING DINNER*, WELLINGTON?
I HAD PEANUT BUTTER SANDWICHES, MIKKI!
I SENT MY TURKEY TO AFRICA TO HELP RELIEVE HUNGER
11-28
MORRIE
©News America Syndicate 1985
HIYA, MIKKI
HI, RALPH! I THOUGHT WELLINGTON SENT YOU TO AFRICA TO HELP RELIEVE HUNGER!

FARLEY Phil Frank

Thanksgiving in San Francisco... a time to gather to remember families in a city of families..
..The nuclear family..
11-28
..the extended family..
..and the overextended family..
St. Anthony's
©Phil (FOOD FOR THOUGHT) Frank

GEECH® by Jerry Bittle

GEECH, WOULD YOU LIKE TO GIVE THANKS?
SURE.
THANKS FOR EVERYTHING. AMEN.
Bittle
© 1985 Universal Press Syndicate
THAT'S IT?
WELL, I THOUGHT EVERYTHING ABOUT COVERED IT.
11-28

FRANK AND ERNEST ®

by Bob Thaves

WORLD HUNGER
THE ARGUMENT FOR HEREDITY OVER ENVIRONMENT GOT A BOOST TODAY.. A GOVERNMENT REPORT SAID POPULATION IS STILL GROWING BUT THERE'S NOT MUCH ENVIRONMENT LEFT.
© 1985 by NEA, Inc.
THAVES 11-28

MIDDLE AGES

by Ron Jaudon

THIS IS OUR FIRST THANKSGIVING WITHOUT EARL IN A LONG WHILE.
JAUDON
©1985, Washington Post Writers Group
I FEEL BAD ABOUT ENJOYING OUR FRIENDSHIP AND MUTUAL GOOD FORTUNE WHEN HE'S ON THE ROAD SELLING MY SPY SOFTWARE.
11-28
WHEREVER HE IS, I'M SURE HE'S GIVING THANKS IN HIS OWN UNIQUE WAY.
I WAS GOING TO COMPLAIN ABOUT THIS BUT SUDDENLY I REMEMBERED ETHIOPIA.

THE BETTER HALF®
By Harris
HARRIS 11-28
Copyright 1985
Cowles Syndicate, Inc.
AFRICAN AID STILL NEEDED

"If people really cared, there'd be enough tears shed to turn all those deserts into farmland."

WINNIE WINKLE
WELL... *EVERYONE'S* PROBLEMS SEEM TO OVERWHELM THEM AT TIMES...
BUT IT HELPS TO REMEMBER THAT THERE ARE THOSE WHO HAVE TO FACE *THEIR* PROBLEMS WITH AN EMPTY STOMACH!
FRANK BOLLE
©1986 Tribune Media Services, Inc
All Rights Reserved

MARVIN

BY TOM ARMSTRONG

GROWL!
W-WHAT WAS THAT?!
I D-DON'T KNOW, B-BUT IT SURE WAS S-SCARY
STORY OF MY LIFE... THE ONLY FRIGHTENING THING ABOUT ME IS MY EMPTY STOMACH
(c) 1985 News America Syndicate
ARMSTRONG
11-28

the AMAZING SPIDER-MAN®

By Stan Lee

SOME WAY TO SPEND THANKS-GIVING! FREEZING ON A WALL WAITING FOR ROMEO AND JULIET TO SPLIT! WELL, IT'S BETTER THAN STARVING IN ETHIOPIA!
LET'S GO, KIDS! TOMORROW'S ANOTHER DAY!
STAN LEE 11-28
COPYRIGHT © 1985 MARVEL COMICS GROUP, DIV. CADENCE INDUSTRIES CORP. ALL RIGHTS RESERVED. DISTRIBUTED BY COWLES SYNDICATE, INC.
AT LAST! SHE'S HEADING INSIDE. BUT--WHY IS BILL JUST STANDING THERE?

Momma By Mell Lazarus

TODAY, MY FAMILY WILL BE HERE FOR OUR ANNUAL THANKSGIVING FEAST...
-TURKEY, STUFFING, YAMS, PEAS, CARROTS, CORN BREAD...
OF COURSE, KEEP IN MIND THAT WHEN I SAY "FAMILY," I MEAN NUCLEAR FAMILY.
THE REST OF THEM, MY EXTENDED FAMILY- MILLIONS OF PEOPLE- HAVE NO FOOD, AND ARE STARVING, IN OTHER PARTS OF THE WORLD.
GIVE A THOUGHT, TODAY, TO THE REST OF YOUR FAMILY. OKAY?
© News America Syndicate 1985
MELL LAZARUS. 11-28

VIRGIL & CO. **BY STEVE ANSUL**

ALSO IN THE NEWS THIS THANKSGIVING, 1985, IS A REPORT IN FROM ADDIS ABABA, ETHIOPIA.
© News America Syndicate, 1985
CHAIRMAN MENGISTU ANNOUNCED THIS MORNING THAT HIS ETHIOPIAN GOVERNMENT HAS TAKEN YET ANOTHER STEP TOWARD PROGRESS IN FAMINE AID EFFORTS FOR HIS PEOPLE...
Ansul 11-28
...ALL EMERGENCY FAMINE RELIEF CAMPS THROUGHOUT ETHIOPIA ARE SCHEDULED TO RECEIVE BILLBOARD-SIZE PORTRAITS OF MARX, ENGELS, & LENIN.

THE BORN LOSER®

by Art Sansom

YOU'RE GIVING MONEY TO "USA FOR AFRICA"?
OF COURSE.
!
THIS IS THE DAY THAT WE WHO "HAVE" SHOULD GIVE TO THOSE WHO "HAVEN'T."
BESIDES, IT'S A TAX WRITE-OFF FOR YOU, RANCID W. VEEBLEFESTER!
© 1985 by NEA, Inc
11-28

STUMPY STUMBLER

by Emil Abrahamian

SOMETIMES I WISH I WAS A HUMAN AND HAD THE CRAVING FOR A JUICY STEAK WITH MUSHROOMS, BAKED POTATOES AND APPLE PIE.
BUT ON THE OTHER HAND, WITH ALL THE STARVATION IN THIS WORLD, I SHOULD BE COMPASSIONATE AND BE CONTENT WITH WHAT I HAVE.
© 1985 Abrahamian Feature Syndicate
EoVo ABRAHAMIAN

GUMDROP ®

by Jerry Scott

SCOTT
11-28

"SINCE WE'RE SHARING OUR FOOD WITH THE HUNGRY PEOPLE IN AFRICA, ARE YOU GOING TO MAKE THEM FINISH THEIR CRANBERRIES, TOO?"

SONS OF LIBERTY

by RICHARD LYNN

FREEDOM FROM HUNGER
USA for AFRICA™
United Support of Artists for Africa
© RICHARD LYNN 1985

TANK McNAMARA®

by Jeff Millar & Bill Hinds

IT'S HALF A CUP OF RICE.
WE GAVE WHAT A THANKSGIVING MEAL WOULD HAVE COST TO FIGHT WORLD HUNGER.
DID SWEATSOX APPROVE?
HE WOULD...
GO FOR IT!
© 1985 Universal Press Syndicate
...IF HE'D NOTICE...
GREAT TURKEY, HON. LOVE THE DRESSING.
NO PANIC. NO PANIC. PLENTY OF TIME LEFT...
MILLAR/HINDS 11-28

BEARS in LOVE®

by Eric Meese

IS EVERYONE GETTING ENOUGH TO EAT?
UH-HUH. BUT I HAVEN'T SEEN BAXTER TAKE A BITE YET.
TRUDY MADE HIM PROMISE TO GIVE EVERYONE A HEAD START SO THE LITTLE ONES WOULD HAVE A CHANCE AT THE GOODIES.
SIGH. IF YOU WANT TO FEED THE MASSES, YOU HAVE TO MAKE A FEW SACRIFICES.
© 1985 Universal Press Syndicate
11-28
E. MEESE

Betty Boop and Felix®

by The Walker Brothers

SORRY I'M LATE, FELIX. I WAS DOING A BENEFIT FOR "USA FOR AFRICA"
MEOW
© 1985 King Features Syndicate, Inc. World rights reserved.
I KNOW YOU'RE HUNGRY...
GROWL
FELIX
11-28
BUT SO ARE MILLIONS OF OTHERS
FELIX
the Walker Bros.

FRED BASSET

BY ALEX GRAHAM

STILL HUNGRY?
Of course!
© Associated Newspapers Group p.l.c. 1985
Dist. News America Syndicate
BUT YOU'VE JUST HAD YOUR DINNER.
What's that got to do with it?
11-28
But I mustn't complain when there are millions starving in Africa.
GRAHAM

WIZARD OF ID

BY BRANT PARKER & JOHNNY HART

YOUR THANKSGIVING SWILL, SPOOKIE! ...I EVEN THREW IN MY OWN WISHBONE!
I CAN'T BELIEVE THIS!
...I ONLY WISH I COULD SHARE SUCH "GENEROUS BOUNTY" WITH YOUR STARVING PEASANTS
11·28
© News America Syndicate, 1985
PARKER

MANDRAKE the MAGICIAN®

By Lee Falk

WHAT SHOULD WE PLAY?
I DUNNO.
PLAY HOUSE.
FALK & FREDERICKS 11-28
END WORLD HUNGER.
MANDRAKE'S MIGHTY MAGIC!
??!!
GOODY! I'LL BE THE MOMMA. YOU BE THE PAPA.
OKAY..
© 1985 King Features Syndicate, Inc. World rights reserved.

love is ...
Kim
11-28
... keeping the family well fed.
TM Reg. U.S. Pat. Off.—all rights reserved
©1985 Los Angeles Times Syndicate

KIT 'N' CARLYLE ® by Larry Wright

WHY COULDN'T I FEEL GUILTY ABOUT ALL THE POOR HUNGRY PEOPLE IN THE WORLD **AFTER** THE THANKSGIVING TURKEY WAS ALL GONE?
CARLYLE
11-28
LARRY WRIGHT
© 1985 by NEA, Inc.

UG!® by Tom Wilson Jr.

HELLO? ANGELO'S PIZZA?— DO YOU DELIVER?—GREAT!— HOW MUCH IS A LARGE PEPPERONI PIZZA?—$10.00?— GREAT! I'VE GOT JUST ENOUGH!—OK, I'D LIKE TO ORD—
$10.00? FOR PIZZA? YOU JUST HAD DINNER, UG!
HOLD ON A SECOND!
USA FOR AFRICA HELPS THOUSANDS
© 1985 Universal Press Syndicate
..AND NOW YOU'RE GOING TO SPEND THAT $10.00 ON SOMETHING THAT YOU DON'T REALLY NEED! DO YOU REALIZE HOW MANY HUNGRY PEOPLE IN AFRICA THAT COULD HELP?
I GUESS YOU'RE RIGHT, BOGEY!
AFRICA NEEDS OUR HELP!
...THEY REALLY DO NEED THIS MORE THAN ME!
HELLO? ANGELO'S?
HOW FAR DO YOU DELIVER?
11-28
WILSON

THE PHANTOM® By Lee Falk & Sy Barry

DROP YOUR GUNS!
!!
END WORLD HUNGER!
©1985 King Features Syndicate, Inc. World rights reserved.
GET OUT AND SHUT THE DOOR BEHIND YOU...
FALK & BARRY 11/28
WE'RE STILL IN CONFERENCE!
NOW WHAT?

SAM and SILO® By Jerry Dumas

POOR LITTLE BIRD. YOU DON'T GET MUCH TO EAT, DO YOU?
11-28
AH, WELL. THERE ARE HUMAN BEINGS BY THE MILLIONS WHO ARE REALLY STARVING.
© 1985 King Features Syndicate, Inc. World rights reserved.
ALL THAT TALK ABOUT STARVING GOT HIM A LITTLE NERVOUS.
dumas

WINTHROP® by Dick Cavalli

WHAT WAS THAT?
MY STOMACH RUMBLED... I'M HUNGRY.
© 1985 by NEA, Inc.
I WAS THINKING ABOUT ESCARGOT WITH POTATOES A L'ARCHIODOISE.
SO THAT'S WHAT A GOURMET STOMACH RUMBLE SOUNDS LIKE.
DICK CAVALLI
11-28

THE GIRLS BY FRANKLIN FOLGER

Dist. News America Syndicate 1985
11-28

"Knowing how you all worry about the famine, I've fixed something you won't feel guilty about eating.

THE Little MAN® by Salmon

When I target a subject for a painting, I make every effort to leave no room for misinterpretation!
WORLD HUNGER
11·28

HI and LOIS®

By Mort Walker & Dik Browne

WHAT'S FOR DESSERT, MOM?
CHOCOLATE CAKE
I THOUGHT YOU SAID WE'RE GOING TO CUT DOWN ON DESSERTS, LOIS
©1985 King Features Syndicate, Inc. World rights reserved.
DIK BROWNE 11-28
WE ARE

RIP KIRBY®

By John Prentice & Fred Dickenson

EVEN OFFICER GILHOOLY OUGHT TO REMEMBER SEEING THIS THING ON THAT FELLOW DESMOND'S COAT.
JOHN PRENTICE 11-28
WHILE SELFISH MEN SET A TRAP...
OTHERS FACE MORE GENEROUS CHORES WITH KIRBY.
OUR LANDLADY HAS INVITED ME TO CARVE FOR THIS SPECIAL TREAT, DESMOND.
CAPITAL, SIR. SHE ALSO PROMISED ME DUMPLINGS.
I TOLD HER WE'D ALL BE GLAD TO SHARE OUR PORTIONS WITH ANYONE WHO NEEDS THEM.
©1985 King Features Syndicate, Inc. World rights reserved.

LUANN

BY GREG EVANS

WHAT'CHA DOIN', LUANN?
I'M SENDING SOME PEOPLE A THANKSGIVING GIFT
A THANKSGIVING GIFT?!! WHO WOULD YOU SEND A THAN-
USA FOR AFRICA
6240 WILSHIRE
SUITE 1900
LOS ANGELES
CA 90048
© News America Syndicate, 1985
11·28
GREG

PERKY & BEANZ

By Russell Myers

PERKY, I'M SENDING FOOD TO THOSE IN NEED. HELP ME SORT OUT THE VERY BEST!
AND THROW OUT THE JUNK?
NO, NO, NO!
BEANZ GREENZ
THAT GOES TO OUR CUSTOMERS JUST LIKE ALWAYS!
AT BEANZ GREENZ IT'S TRADITION THAT COUNTS!!
© 1985 Tribune Media Services, Inc
All Rights Reserved
RUSSELL MYERS
11/28

JUDGE PARKER

BY PAUL NICHOLS

ABBEY, DID YOU EVER SEE ANYONE WHO WAS STARVING?
NOT REALLY! WHY DO YOU ASK, SARA?
I WAS THINKING THAT IF YOU DID, I'D LIKE TO GIVE THEM MY DINNER TONIGHT!
HAROLD LEDOUX 11-28
©News America Syndicate, 1985
YOU KNOW,...IF EVERYONE FELT AS YOU DO, NO PERSON ON THIS EARTH WOULD EVER STARVE AGAIN!

THE EVERMORES®

By Johnny Sajem

THIS IS TRULY A WORTHY CAUSE, TITUS, YOU MUST HELP!
BUT I ALWAYS KICK PEOPLE OUT! I WON'T BREAK MY RECORD!
WE ARE THE WORLD, WE ARE THE CHILDREN
11-28
© 1985 King Features Syndicate, Inc. World rights reserved.
SAJEM

GARFIELD® by Jim Davis

GARFIELD, YOU EAT FOOD LIKE IT GROWS ON TREES
I WASN'T BORN YESTERDAY. I KNOW THE FOOD FAIRY BRINGS IT IN THE NIGHT
GARFIELD
JIM DAVIS
© 1985 United Feature Syndicate, Inc.
WHAT IF THE FOOD JUST STOPPED?
I COULD HANDLE THAT
GARFIELD
IT'S THE EATING I WOULD MISS
GARFIELD
11-28

CONRAD By Bill Schorr

ISN'T IT AWFUL ABOUT ALL THOSE STARVING PEOPLE IN AFRICA?...
YEAH...MY COUSIN VOLUNTEERED TO HELP FEED THEM...
SO DID MINE...
MY COUSIN'S A RED CROSS NURSE...
© 1985 Tribune Media Services, Inc. All Rights Reserved
MINE'S A HOT CROSS BUN...
11-28

Village Square by Chuck Stiles

USA for AFRICA
CHUCK STILES

"RELATIVELY SPEAKING, WE'RE REALLY QUITE THANKFUL..."

ADventures™ by Vadun

HELP WANTED
USA for AFRICA
United Support of Artists for Africa
11/28
VADUN
© 1985 United Feature Syndicate, Inc.

KUDZU

By Doug Marlette

IF I COULD JUST GET TINA AND MICK TO APPEAR ON MY THANKSGIVING TELETHON...
..I COULD DO SO MUCH WITH THE MONEY WE'D RAISE TO MAKE THIS PLANET A BETTER PLACE TO LIVE!
MARLETTE
11/28
LIKE FEEDING THE HUNGRY IN AFRICA?
AMEN!
..PLUS, INSTALLING A JACUZZI IN OUR BAPTISMAL POOL!
©Jefferson Communications, Inc. 1985
Distributed by Tribune Media Services, Inc.

EB AND FLO ®

by Paul Sellers

IT'S A FOUR-LETTER WORD
© 1985 United Feature Syndicate, Inc.
11-28
YOU CAN EAT IT
I WANT SOME
WHAT IS IT?

For Better or For Worse®

by Lynn Johnston

LINEUPS OF WOMEN AND CHILDREN WAIT FOR THEIR ONE CUP OF MILK... MANY TOO WEAK TO STAND.
FAMINE
11-28
© 1985 Universal Press Syndicate
UNABLE TO FIND ENOUGH FOOD, PEOPLE ARE DIGGING INTO ANT HILLS HOPING TO FIND RICE THAT MAY HAVE BEEN CARRIED IN BY....
FAMINE
WHAT'S FOR SUPPER, MOM? WE'RE STARVING!!
LYNN

APARTMENT 3-G

BY ALEX KOTZKY

I HOPE YOU MEN ARE READY FOR A BREAK! THE DELI JUST SENT UP SANDWICHES, MILK AND COFFEE! IT ISN'T EXACTLY A THANKSGIVING DINNER---BUT IT'LL HAVE TO DO!
MILK
11-28 © News America Syndicate, 1985
THERE ARE PEOPLE THROUGHOUT THE WORLD WHO DON'T GET THIS MUCH TO EAT IN A MONTH, LET ALONE A SINGLE NIGHT! AS INDIVIDUALS WE MUST FIND A WAY TO HELP!
MILK
ALEX KOTZKY

Doonesbury

BY GARRY TRUDEAU

OKAY, THE BOYS AND ME IS GONNA TAKE A TURKEY BREAK, BUT DON'T GO AWAY!
THUMPA! THUMPA!
COULD I HAVE SECONDS AND THIRDS WITH MY FIRSTS, PLEASE?
NOT TO WORRY. TODAY THERE'S PLENTY.
© 1985 G. B. Trudeau
UNIVERSAL PRESS SYNDICATE
11-28
SO YOU THINK HUNGER HAS INCREASED DRAMATICALLY IN THE LAST FEW YEARS, ALICE?
HEY, THE STORIES I COULD TELL YOU, MARV!
HEAR THAT? I **KNEW** HUNGER WAS ANECDOTAL!
YES, DEAR.
NPR
URBAN HOME COMPANION
GBTrudeau

ARCHIE ®

HI! DINNER IS ALREADY ON THE TABLE!
11-28
© 1985 King Features Syndicate, Inc. World rights reserved.
YOUR DINNER GUEST IS HERE, DAD!
HE CALLED AN HOUR AGO AND SAID HE COULDN'T MAKE IT!
THEY SURE TREAT SALESMEN NICE IN THIS HOUSE!

the neighborhood™ Jerry Van Amerongen

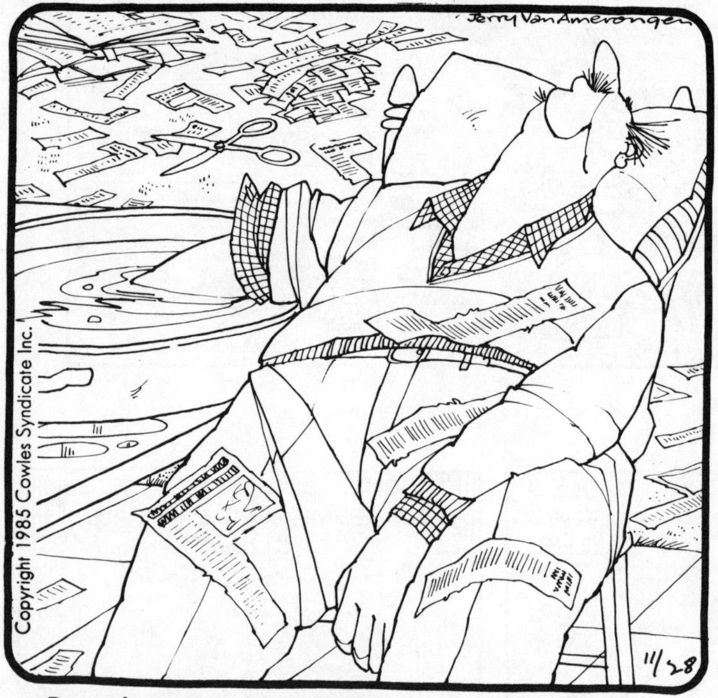
Jerry Van Amerongen
Copyright 1985 Cowles Syndicate Inc.
11/28

Ben thought it might be interesting to clip articles that located areas of hunger in the world . . . until, of course, his clipping hand seized-up.

TRUDY

11-28
Dear grandma-
I had a nice Thanks-giving dinner. Turkey with stuffing! Mom tells me some kids in the world didn't have any Turkey today. That's hard to believe!
Love, Crawford xx
P.S.
I hope they at least had Cranberry Sauce!
© 1985 King Features Syndicate, Inc. World rights reserved.
jerry marcus

NUBBIN®

By Boltinoff and Burnett

I WISH I HAD ENOUGH FOOD
TO FEED A MILLION HUNGRY FOLKS IN THE WORLD.
WISHING WELL
11-28
BOLTINOFF BURNETT
COULD YOU MAKE THAT A MILLION AND **ONE** ?

SECRET AGENT CORRIGAN®

By George Evans

A GREAT SAILING SHIP FULL OF ARMED MEN HAS ANCHORED OFF THE SOUTHERN COAST.
ON HELMETS AND COLLARS THERE ARE SYMBOLS...
OUCH! *THEY* WON'T BACK AWAY. MY PEOPLE AND I MUST DEFEND THE "GODDESS".
SPEARS... AGAINST ASSAULT RIFLES, ROCKETS, GRENADES, CHIEF?
11-28
JOIN THE WORLD FIGHT AGAINST HUNGER! Phil Corrigan
GEORGE EVANS

HARTLAND®

by Rich Torrey

DAD...DOESN'T IT BOTHER YOU THAT WE'RE ABLE TO GET FOOD ANY TIME OUR LITTLE HEART'S DESIRE...WHILE THROUGHOUT THE WORLD MILLIONS OF PEOPLE ARE STARVING?
...DOESN'T IT MAKE YOU WANT TO DO SOMETHING ABOUT IT? TO HELP OUT IN SOME WAY?!... HUH?!...
CAN I TAKE YOUR ORDER?
YEA! 60 MILLION CHEESE-BURGERS!...AND PLEASE HURRY!!
FEEL BETTER?
WOULD YOU LIKE ANYTHING TO DRINK WITH THAT?
PHEW
11-28

BRICK BRADFORD®

By Paul Norris

WHAT'S HER PROBLEM? TOO MUCH RADIATION? DOES SHE HAVE SOME SORT OF ILLNESS?
WHEN DID SHE LAST EAT? SHE'S SUFFER-ING FROM AN UNWHOLE-SOME CONDITION....
SHE'S WEAK FROM HUNGER!
Paul NORRIS 11-28

AMY®
By Jack Tippit
Copyright 1985
Cowles Syndicate, Inc.
11-28
Jack Tippit

"Mom, I'll be happy to donate MY broccoli to all the hungry children of the world!"

Ben Wicks
MORE
ROCK
STARS
VISIT
ETHIOPIA
Wicks

"You'd have thought they'd suffered enough."

Barney Google and Snuffy Smith

By Fred Lasswell

AWK! THIS DADBURN SOUP'S TOO ALL-FIRED HOT
NO WONDER!! IT HASN'T BEEN BLESSED YET
FRED LASSWELL
11-28

TUMBLEWEEDS

BY TOM K. RYAN

THIS THANKSGIVING GOD WANTS US TO SHARE OUR FOOD WITH STARVING PEOPLE ALL OVER THE WORLD.
HE DOES?
YES, AND THAT'S NOT EASY.
IT'S NOT?
JUST TRY ADDRESSING AN ENVELOPE WITH A TURKEY DRUMSTICK INSIDE OF IT.
© News America Syndicate, 1985
11-28
T.K. RYAN

by Robert Gill

IT'S NOT A LOT TO GIVE AND IT'S ALL I'VE GOT... BUT MAYBE IT'LL HELP!
WE'LL ENJOY OUR DINNER WHEN WE KNOW SOMEONE WHO'S HUNGRY IS ENJOYING THANKSGIVING TOO!
I'M PROUD THAT YOU'RE MY BROTHER!
HAPPY THANKSGIVING BIG SISTER!
© National Features Syndicate, 1985
11-28
SUGAR

PEACHES **By Paul Ullrich**

FACE FRONT, TURKEYS! IT'S USA FOR AFRICA TELETHON TIME!
HORRORS! IT'S UNCLE BOYD! PUBLIC TV'S HATCHET MAN!
ONCE AGAIN, WE HAVE SHOWS SO BAD THAT YOU'LL DIG DEEP INTO YOUR WALLETS AND PLEDGE MONEY JUST TO END THE PAIN!
REMEMBER OUR NANCY SINATRA FILM FESTIVAL? BRACE YOURSELVES...
FOR WHO? JOEY HEATHERTON? CHARO?
....FOR THE JOE NAMATH FILM FESTIVAL!
ARRGH!
© 1985 COPLEY NEWS SERVICE

BLONDIE®

by Dean Young and Stan Drake

TONIGHT I'M MAKING A LITTLE SANDWICH AS A GESTURE FOR THE WORLD'S HUNGRY
THAT'S NICE, HONEY
THAT'S A LITTLE SANDWICH ?
OF COURSE IT'S LITTLE
TWO ARMS IS A BIG SANDWICH
STRANGELY ENOUGH, FOR HIM IT MAKES SENSE
11-28
YOUNG DRAKE

QUINCY®

By Ted Shearer

BOUNCY, IF YOU HAD TWO WISHES, WHAT WOULD THEY BE ?
A TURKEY DINNER FOR EVERY-ONE OF THOSE HUNGRY AFRICAN CHILDREN...
...AN TWO EXTRA HELPIN'S OF TURKEY AND GRAVY FOR ME.
11-28
TED SHEARER

DOLLAR$ AND NONENE®

MANKOFF
© 1985 United Feature Syndicate Inc

HEALTH CAPSULES®
by Michael A. Petti, M.D.

HOW COMMON IS MALNUTRITION IN YOUNG CHILDREN IN AFRICA DURING DROUGHT-FREE PERIODS?

11-28
JUD
HURD
AFRIC

ON THE AVERAGE 25% SUFFER MALNUTRITION, OFTEN RESULTING IN PERMANENT BRAIN DAMAGE AND STUNTING OF GROWTH.

Health Capsules gives helpful information.
It is not intended to be of a diagnostic nature.

DUFFY® by BRUCE HAMMOND

YOU KNOW, THERE ARE MILLIONS OF HUNGRY PEOPLE WHO NEED THAT SANDWICH MORE THAN YOU DO, DUFFY!
© 1985 Universal Press Syndicate
YOU'RE RIGHT, NAOMI.
CAN I KEEP THE PICKLE?
HAMMOND
11-28

LITTLE FARMER By KERN PEDERSON

CEMEN
AL SMITH FEATURE SERVICE
KERN
SUPPORT
USA FOR
AFRICA
11-28-'85

BROOM-HILDA

by Russell Myers

IRWIN, WE'VE SPENT WEEKS COLLECTING FOOD FOR NEEDY PEOPLE...
NOW WE MUST INSURE THAT EVERY BITE ARRIVES SAFELY!
RUSSELL MYERS 11/28

GIL THORP

by Jack Berrill

NOT ONE OF OUR BETTER SCRIMMAGES, GIL!
NOPE... BEATING TECH WASN'T ON THEIR MINDS THIS MORNING!
11/28
1985 Tribune Media Services, Inc. All Rights Reserved
OH, MAN... I'M STARVED... I CAN'T WAIT TO DIG INTO THAT BIRD AN' ALL THE FIXIN'S!
YEAH... IT'S "PIG OUT" TIME FOR EVERYBODY!
NOT FOR EVERYBODY, FELLAS!
FIGHT WORLD FAMINE
BERRILL

TYLER TWO

by Leslie Harris

QUIT GRIPING, SAMMY! TURKEY IS AN AMERICAN TRADITION.
ONE THAT I COULD LIVE WITHOUT!
FINE! LET'S CHUCK THE BIRD AND MAKE OURS AN INTERNATIONAL THANKSGIVING!
LESLIE
11-28
YEAH!
TODAY WE'LL CELEBRATE LIKE ETHIOPIANS!
WHAT DO THEY DO?
© 1985 Tribune Media Services, Inc. All Rights Reserved
STARVE.
FOOD FOR THOUGHT.
I'LL JUST EAT MY WORDS, THANKS.

BUGS BUNNY ®

by Warner Bros.

!
© 1985 by Warner Bros Inc All Rights Reserved
YOU NO-GOOD WABBIT. I WAS GOING TO SEND THOSE CAWWOTS TO STARVING AFWICANS.
THAT'S WHERE I'M TAKING THEM, DOC.
Distributed by NEA Inc
I GUESS HE ISN'T ***ALL BAD***, AFTER ALL.
11-28

REX MORGAN, M.D. BY DAL CURTIS

THANKSGIVING IS A DAY TO GIVE THANKS FOR OUR BLESSINGS!
IT'S ALSO A DAY FOR EACH OF US TO GIVE--- SO THAT OTHERS, LESS FORTUNATE, MAY SHARE IN THOSE BLESSINGS!
BRADLEY and EDGINGTON 11-28
©News America Syndicate, 1985
DiPreta

THE SMITH FAMILY® By Mr. and Mrs. George Smith

11-28
© 1985 Universal Press Syndicate
REMEMBER THE HUNGRY PEOPLE OF AFRICA, MOM.
VIRGINIA + GEORGE